STRESS & DEPRESSION

Sarah Lennard-Brown

HODDER
Wayland

an imprint of Hodder Children's Books

White-Thomson Publishing Ltd,
2-3 St Andrew's Place, Lewes,
East Sussex BN7 1UP

Published in Great Britain in 2001 by Hodder Wayland, an imprint of Hodder Children's Books

This book was produced for White-Thomson Publishing Ltd by Ruth Nason.

Design: Carole Binding
Picture research: Glass Onion Pictures

The right of Sarah Lennard-Brown to be identified as the author of this work has been asserted by her in accordance with the Copyright, Designs and Patents Act 1988.

British Library Cataloguing in Publication Data
Lennard-Brown, Sarah
   Stress & Depression. - (Health Issues)
   1. Depression, Mental - Juvenile literature
   2. Stress (Psychology) - Juvenile literature
   I. Title
   616.8'527

ISBN 0 7502 3182 3

616·8527
BRO

Printed in Italy by G. Canale & C.S.p.A.

Hodder Children's Books
A division of Hodder Headline Limited
338 Euston Road, London NW1 3BH

Acknowledgements
The author thanks Ray and Maureen Lennard-Brown and Matthew Williams for their help, advice and encouragement; and Rebecca Williams for help with the resources. The author and publishers thank the following for their permission to reproduce photographs and illustrations: Corbis Images: pages 7 (Paul A. Souders), 9 (Wartenberg/Picture Press), 13 (top) (Kelly Harriger), 14 (Gilbert Lundt; TempSport), 17 (Leng/Leng), 21 (Neil Rabinowitz), 22 (Tim Wright), 32 (Lawrence Manning), 34 (Jenny Woodcock; Reflections Photolibrary), 54 (Richard T. Nowitz); Angela Hampton Family Life Pictures: pages 8, 11, 13 (bottom), 26, 29, 30, 31, 35, 36, 38, 40, 43, 46, 50 (top), 53; Photofusion: pages 6 (Bob Watkins), 15 (Mark Campbell), 19 (Christa Stadtler), 27 (Don Gray), 28 (Mark Campbell), 41 (Gina Glover), 47 (Paul Doyle), 48 (Gina Glover), 50 (bottom) (Don Gray), 52 (Ray Roberts); Pictorial Press Ltd: pages 18 (20th Century Fox), 20 (© Polygram); Popperfoto: pages 4, 10, 16; Wayland Picture Library: cover, and pages 1 and 42 (Tizzie Knowles) and pages 37 (Chris Fairclough), 4 (Michael Courtney), 56. The life events stress scores on page 21 are reprinted from the **Journal of Psychosomatic Research**, Vol. 11, 1967, Holmes et al, *Social Readjustment Rating Scale*, with permission from Elsevier Science.

Contents

Introduction
Stress and depression

Stress and depression are both fascinating subjects to investigate. This book aims to give an insight into what they are, how they can affect you and how to manage and treat them.

Stress is part of our everyday lives. We hear or read about it all the time, on the television, Internet and radio, and in newspapers and magazines. People even sing songs about stress. People talk about stress at work or being 'stressed out' by their parents. Magazines warn of the dangers of stress during family holidays or exams. Often people say they are stressed when they are talking about things that worry them, or when they feel under pressure and unable to cope with a situation.

There are lots of different ideas about stress. Even the experts can't agree. In this book we will use the most commonly accepted view, which sees stress as being all about change and the way each individual reacts to change. So, what is a stressful change for one person will not be for another. It is the change itself that is the stress (sometimes called a stressor). Whether it is harmful to us depends on our individual personality, the support of the people around us and how we have learnt to cope with different changes.

Stress and depression are linked. If you experience too much stress you are at risk of developing depression. If you suffer from depression you certainly experience a lot of stress. Depression is a medical illness that is usually triggered by some form of stress. It affects over 1 in 10 of the adult population and can be fatal. According to the World Health Organization, depression will be one of the most important health issues of the 21st century.

A stress ball

A stressed employee on the Swiss stock market kneads a 'stress ball'. Many such 'executive toys' are designed to help relieve stress.

Bank Managers' Stress Payout is tip of the iceberg

America's latest export: a stressed-out world

Ideas about stress and depression are constantly changing. Recently scientists have begun to map out how stress and depression change the chemicals in our brains. This has produced lots of new ideas about what happens when people suffer from too much stress or depression.

In this book we start by investigating the link between stress and change. Then we look at what happens when you experience stress, and explore some ideas about how to manage stress. In the second part of the book we answer the question 'what is depression?', then look at what happens when you are depressed, its signs and symptoms and the facts about suicide. We end with an investigation into different ways of treating and beating depression.

Stress kills dot.com flyer

When stress enters the germ equation

Stressed-out brides more likely to get divorced, say psychologists

Childhood abuse and adult stress

Stressful work doubles risk of premature birth

Stress-free Scots score own goal

Surfing the net at home makes you depressed

Stress turns school into climate of fear

Elderly veteran is treated for battle stress

Study hints mental, not physical, stress is bigger heart problem

1 Stress and change
The types of change we all experience

Stress means different things to different people. Everyone has their own view of stress, even the experts. The most commonly accepted view of stress was developed by Richard Lazarus, an American psychologist, in 1966. He felt that stress was all about change and that each individual responds to changes (he called changes 'stressors')

Happy birthday
Family celebrations can sometimes be very stressful.

in a unique way. This means that any change in your life, your mind, your friends and family, your body or your environment is, to some extent, stressful. Getting married, worrying about money, arguing with your friends or catching a cold all involve change and so are stressful.

The important thing to remember is that any change is stressful – good changes as well as bad ones. A surprise birthday party, passing exams, winning some money, even lying in the sun are all examples of pleasurable things that can cause stress. Going to a party, passing exams and winning money all cause excitement and worry, whilst sunbathing can cause your skin stress from overheating.

Even imagining change can be stressful. For example, thinking about what life would be like if someone you love fell ill, or what you would do if you became very poor, or even what would happen if you became very rich, all involve worrying. Worrying about changes whether they are good or bad is stressful.

Fans
Being a fan can be exciting and enjoyable and stressful.

Examples of things that cause stress

Good things

Surprise birthday party
Scoring the winning goal
Passing exams
Holidays
Family celebrations
Meeting deadlines
Winning money
Falling in love
Moving house

Bad things

Being ill
Missing the goal
Failing exams
Traffic delays
Family celebrations
Work deadlines
Debt
Arguments
Moving house

Reliving the glory

You should have seen me in the game last week. It was brilliant! Two minutes to go and we had one goal all. Then Harry (he's on the wing) passed me a beauty right in front of an open goal, and I scored. It was fantastic! The crowd cheered for ages and the rest of the team were all over me, jumping on my back. The game was four days ago and I can't stop thinking about it. I can't sleep. I just keep reliving it – you know, playing it again. It was great but I keep thinking, will I be able to do it again? They'll expect it every time now. Normal life seems a bit flat now.
(David, soccer player, 15 years old)

Hayfever

Hayfever is one example of a physical change that causes stress.

Physical changes

Stressful physical changes include illness, allergies, puberty, pregnancy, drug use and violence. All of these involve a change in the state of your body and so they are all stressful. When your body is ill, or has an allergic reaction, it has to fight infection and repair the damage. Drugs, such as tobacco, alcohol and caffeine, all result in changes in body chemistry; then the substances have to be eliminated and the damage repaired. Violence or accidental injury also mean that your body has to work hard repairing the damage.

Changes that happen at puberty

Boys

Muscle growth

Grow taller

Voice gets deeper

Growth of body hair

Growth of facial hair

Growth of hair around penis

Penis and testes enlarge

Sperm mature and become active

Pores enlarge

Skin becomes more oily (spots and acne)

Mood swings

Tiredness

Irritability

Girls

Menstruation (periods) begins

Pregnancy is now possible

Breasts develop and grow

Body hair grows under arms and in pubic area

Grow taller

Pelvis gets wider

Fatty deposits around the body

Pores enlarge

Skin becomes more oily (spots and acne)

Mood swings

Tiredness

Irritability

Hormonal changes occur throughout life and can be a major cause of physical stress. The hormonal changes that happen at puberty in males and females (usually between ages 10 and 16) are very stressful as they involve changes in body shape and function. The hormones that cause these changes are testosterone in males and a mixture of hormones including oestrogen and progesterone in females.

For both sexes puberty can involve mood swings and irritability. It causes skin pores to enlarge and become oilier, especially on the nose and forehead. This can result in spots and acne, a change that most people find very stressful.

Pregnancy causes enormous body changes, and childbirth can be severely stressful because of the sudden drop in the mother's hormone levels. Women can also experience stress due to the hormonal changes that occur before a period or at menopause.

Stress occurs when you push your body too hard. For example, if you are working hard all day and then staying out late at night, you are reducing the amount of time your body has to restore itself during sleep. If these changes are added to by puberty, or a dose of hayfever, or smoking cigarettes, your body has to fight hard to stay healthy. If your body has to endure too many changes you may end up becoming ill from too much stress.

Teenage stress
Physical and emotional changes at puberty are causes of stress.

Psychological changes

Psychological changes involve the thoughts, feelings, memories and emotions that go on inside your head. Any change – real or imagined – can be stressful. So worrying about things that haven't happened yet, or getting anxious about events in the past or the future, is stressful.

Grief can cause an enormous amount of psychological change as you come to terms with it, whether the grief is for the loss of a parent, a close family member, or a friend. Loss of a loved pet or a treasured possession or a job can also cause grief and stress. Sometimes this can be overwhelming.

Shared grief
Three friends comfort each other at a funeral in Israel.

Other psychological stressors (changes) include rejection, fear, anger, resentment, criticism (both from yourself and others), and feelings of sexuality and frustration. Feeling powerless can also be very stressful, as there can seem to be no way out of the problem and no end to it. It is very important to talk to someone about these feelings, as a trusted individual outside a situation can very often help.

It is not only negative or sad feelings that can result in stress. Good feelings can also be stressful: love, for example. The feeling experienced when first falling in love is intense. Again, it is a situation that involves change and is therefore stressful. Feelings such as anticipation, excitement and hope are pleasurable but are also stressful.

Sam, sleepless and heart sore

Sam is seventeen. He has recently split up with his girlfriend, Kelly, who had started to see someone else. Sam feels terrible. He can't sleep, but he feels very tired. He doesn't want to get out of bed at all. He feels angry and sad and hurt in turns and sometimes he doesn't know what he feels. He started a fight with his best friend just for the excuse to hit someone. His mum is worried that he will get in trouble with the police. His dad has planned a weekend away fishing to try to cheer him up. He remembers feeling just like Sam when he was younger and he hopes that, if he and Sam get away from it all for a little while, Sam will be able to come to terms with his loss and remember how much he loves fishing.

New love

Falling in love causes many kinds of feelings, all of which cause stress.

Spiritual changes

Spiritual or religious experiences can also be stressful. Whether you are being converted to a new religion, finding faith or questioning your faith, all these things involve change and therefore stress. Admitting to having a faith can be stressful, especially if your faith involves some form of outward sign that is unfamiliar to the people you mix with, such as special clothing. However, having a strong faith and a supportive religious community can also help you to overcome stress. People who are members of a religious community often seem to suffer less from stress-related illness. Some researchers feel that this is a result of being part of a supportive community, but the individuals themselves feel that it also has something to do with their beliefs.

Social changes

Working long hours week in, week out without a break can cause too much stress. Not working at all can also be stressful. Unemployment has many consequences for people, including stress caused by changes in social situation. This is especially true for men whose whole circle of friends can be work-related (more common in western countries than other parts of the world).

Other social stressors (changes) can be moving to a new school, meeting unfamiliar people, arguments with family and friends, competition at work or school, bullying and cultural change. Pressure from friends to conform to their way of behaving, and pressure from advertising to spend more than you can afford, or to attain a certain body image, can also be stressful. Stress occurs even in positive social situations such as starting a new job, or getting married. The stress experienced in competitive situations can be positive. It can be exciting, exhilarating and inspire you to perform better.

'Being made redundant was a terrible experience. I'd worked so hard for years and it was all gone. Just like that. I felt numb, shocked. It really rocked me.'
(Mike, unemployed car mechanic)

Facing up to the bullies

Hi, I'm just off to get a burger with Mum. It's a treat she's been planning because we're celebrating. Nothing spectacular. I managed to go to school for a whole week without bunking off. The teachers were really pleased, too. I haven't been for about a term. It was nice to have them all pleased with me for once. At first they got really mad with me, about not going to school and everything. They kept asking me why? But I couldn't tell them. I was so scared and ashamed. Some girls in my class beat me up, stole my money, that sort of thing. It got so that I couldn't sleep or eat. Then I started talking about it to Mark at the youth club, and it changed everything. He encouraged me to tell Mum and she talked to the teachers at school. They arranged for me to talk to other people who had suffered the same sort of thing and life got easier. So here I am. It's still difficult, but I'm getting there and I'm not going to let them beat me this time.
(Rachael, 13 years old)

Environmental changes

Our surroundings can be a big source of stress. If conditions are too hot or too cold your body reacts in order to protect itself from damage. If you are too cold, your body will start shivering to try to warm you up. If you are too hot, your body will start sweating in order to cool you down. If these responses don't work, damage can occur.

Other forms of environmental stress include pollution, dust, damp, poisons and infections. All of these can cause changes in your body and are therefore stressful.

Environmental stress

Change in altitude is a form of environmental stress, and living in poor, damp housing is another, less pleasant, one. Having someone to talk to makes stress easier to cope with.

Throughout this chapter we have looked at the different sorts of stressors (changes) we experience every day. In the next chapter we will investigate what happens to you when you are stressed. We will look at the problems stress can cause, who it affects and how it works.

2 What happens when you are stressed?
Why responses differ

As we have seen, anything that causes change is stressful. Just about everything in life causes us some degree of stress, good things as well as bad. In fact, stress is vital to life: without it we would be lifeless blobs; without the stress of hunger we would not eat; without the stress of pain we would not know that we had an injury. So stress is not all bad news. It helps us to keep healthy, awake, alert and active. Stress can be enjoyable and exciting – dancing at parties, running a race, winning, loving. Problems begin when we experience too much stress.

Too much stress is not good for us. It can cause problems in all aspects of our lives. It can cause physical illnesses such as heart disease, irritable bowel syndrome, stroke and ulcers. It can also trigger the development of serious conditions such as alcohol and drug addiction, or eating disorders. Too much stress can make existing problems, such as family arguments, worse. It can also result in severe mental illnesses such as depression.

If you think that you may be suffering from too much stress you should talk about your worries to a doctor or health professional.

Positive stress
In sport, the stress of competition can inspire those taking part to perform even better than normal.

Too much stress can cause ...

Physical problems

Tiredness during the day
Difficulty going to sleep
Frequent waking at night
Aches and pains
Increased number of infections
Palpitations (heart racing)
High blood pressure
Heart attacks
Stroke
Diarrhoea
Constipation
Irritable bowel syndrome
Stomach cramps
Stomach ulcers
Dental problems (due to
excessive teeth grinding)
Mouth ulcers
Skin problems
Menstrual problems
Hormonal imbalances

Psychological problems

Vivid dreams
Lack of interest in the world
Lack of motivation
Listlessness
Irritability
Tearfulness
Anxiety
Poor performance at work
or school
Eating problems (too much
or too little)
Poor self image
Lack of patience
Depression

Social problems

Increasing arguments at
home
Tendency to avoid people
Abuse of alcohol, cigarettes
and other drugs
Increased aggression
(particularly young men)
Inappropriate behaviour
Over-reaction to problems
Ignoring problems

Aggression
*Stress can make
you feel aggressive.*

Worrying times at the social security

Anne has a job in a local social security department. She enjoyed her job at first. She felt she was helping people and making a difference. Then the government cut the department's budgets. Difficult decisions had to be made over which she had no control. She was responsible for telling people that help was no longer available. Anne found this very stressful. Some of the cases kept her awake at night worrying. She started getting stomach pains and neck pains. Her periods became very heavy and she cried a lot. Anne felt she couldn't cope any more. Her doctor told her she is suffering from too much stress, to take a holiday and learn some relaxation exercises. The nurse at work offered her some counselling sessions. Anne has had enough and is looking for a new job.

Individual differences

Different people respond to stressful situations in different ways. Changes that result in too much stress in one person may not affect another person. According to some researchers, approximately one person in ten has a very low stress threshold (tolerance level), and will feel overwhelmed and distressed by normal everyday life.

Many factors affect the way you respond to stress as an individual. These include your genetic makeup, personality type, culture, religion, family and social background, health, environment and life events.

Is your personality...

Type A or ...

Never late
Competitive
Anticipate what others are going to say
High achiever
Impatient
Tense
Tackle more than one task at a time
Emphatic in speech
Care about others' opinions
Quick
Driven

Genetic factors

There is some evidence that an individual's response to stress is genetically inherited from their parents. This is an area that is very hard to research, as it is difficult to work out which responses are inherited genetically and which are learnt. However it seems that your tendency to experience feelings and emotions is to some extent based on your genes. This is especially true for emotions such as anxiety and anger and feelings such as warmth and friendliness.

Other genetic factors that affect your vulnerability to stress include general health, inheritable diseases, life expectancy and appearance. If such a genetic factor gives you a tendency to stress, it is not the end of the world. Factors like these are just one of many things that affect the way an individual responds to change, and therefore their impact can be relatively small.

Type B?

Relaxed about time keeping
Not competitive
Good listener
Balanced approach to achievement
Good at waiting in queues
Relaxed
Take one step at a time
Slow deliberate speech
Self-reliant
Slow
Easy-going

Personality type

Every individual has a unique personality. Investigating personality is difficult because everyone is so different. As a result there are many different theories about how personalities work. One theory that is particularly useful in understanding stress is called a 'Type theory'. Two American doctors, Meyer Friedman and Ray Rosenman, developed the 'Type' theory of personality in 1974, while they were studying people with heart disease. They noticed that many people with heart disease behaved in similar

Differences

People with Type A personalities tend to suffer from more stress-related illnesses. People who can relax properly are better able to manage stress.

ways. They were very competitive, restless, impatient and tense. They labelled this type of personality 'Type A'. 'Type Bs' are the opposite of 'Type As'; they are laid-back, uncompetitive, relaxed and able to take life easy. Friedman and Rosenman thought that people with Type A personalities were more likely to suffer from stress-related illnesses, as they found it difficult to relax. The descriptions of Type A and Type B personalities are extremes. Most people have personalities somewhere between the two; only about 10 per cent of the population have extreme Type A personalities.

Social factors

Humans are social beings and the way we interact with the people around us can have a big impact on how we respond to stress. The way we interact with the people we meet is very complex. It involves our own personalities, the personalities of the people we live, work and play with, our culture, religion, friends and family structure.

Broadly speaking, the more harmonious and relaxed our relationships with the people we live with, the better able we are to cope with stress. Having a close, loving family and a few good friends can help us to cope with the demands of day-to-day living. Living in a family that is abusive, or having friends who are not supportive, can be very stressful.

Health

Your state of health has a profound effect on your

Family life
Many movies and TV programmes are about the stresses of family life. 'The Simpsons' (drawn by Matt Groening) is one example.

ability to tolerate stress. It is far easier to relax and get a sense of perspective on a situation if you are fit, healthy and well rested. Life is harder to cope with if you are disabled, if you have a persistent condition such as asthma or even if you have a cold. Stress levels may well be increased by some chronic conditions such as asthma, eczema, heart disease or diabetes. Even something as simple as not getting enough sleep can decrease your stress tolerance levels.

Your psychological state of health also has a large impact on your stress tolerance level. You are much more likely to suffer from too much stress if you already have a psychological problem such as mental illness, anxiety, low self-esteem, poor body image, or communication difficulties.

Life in the fast lane

Yeh, stress – tell me about it! I know all about the effects of too much stress. At least, I do now. I'd been at college for about a term when it finally got to me. Looking back, it's easy to see what was going on. Leaving home, new town, new college, new friends, freedom, late nights drinking, lots of hard work studying as well as a bar job to keep the debts down. On top of all that I'm diabetic. It's my weak spot. When things get out of balance it gets out of control. So I ended up in hospital. Too much stress the doc said. I'm not doing that again. Not that I'm letting diabetes rule my life. I'm just learning when to pull back a bit, keeping cool.
(Gary, 19 years old)

College friends
Starting college is a stressful time of many new experiences.

Marriage

Getting married is high on the list of stressful life events, but even restful summer holidays have some impact.

Life events

It is well-known that some changes in your life are more stressful than others. Events such as the death of a close friend or relative, being suspended from school or moving house can be particularly challenging. Major changes like these have long-term effects on your life. They are not experienced and then immediately overcome. Their effect is rather like that of a large stone thrown into a pond. The first splash is the biggest but the ripples continue for a long time after the initial impact.

The impact of several big changes in your life can build up over a period of time to cause too much stress. The aim of the life events table (page 21) is to give you an idea of the amount of 'life stress' you are experiencing at the present time. Add up the values of any events that have occurred in your life over the last year. If your score is over 250 and you have normal stress tolerance levels then you may well be experiencing the symptoms associated with too much stress. If you have a low stress tolerance level, then a score of 150 may mean you have experienced enough stress to make you ill.

If you feel you are suffering from too much stress you should talk to your family doctor or other appropriate health professional. In chapter 3 you will find some information on how to manage stress.

STRESS SCORES OF LIFE EVENTS

Death of spouse 100

Divorce 73

Separation...65

Jail term..63

Death of a close family member...........................63

Personal injury or illness.....................................53

Marriage..50

Fired from work or expelled from school............47

Marital reconciliation..45

Retirement...45

Change in health of family member.....................44

Pregnancy..40

Sexual difficulties..39

Gain of a new family member..............................39

Business readjustment...38

Change in financial state.....................................38

Death of a close friend..37

Change to a different line of work.......................36

Change in number of arguments with spouse........35

A large mortgage or loan......................................30

Foreclosure of mortgage or loan..............................30

Change in responsibilities at work.........................29

Son or daughter leaving home...............................29

Trouble with in-laws...29

Outstanding personal achievement........................28

Spouse begins or stops work.................................26

Beginning or end of school or college....................26

Change in living conditions....................................25

Change in personal habits......................................24

Trouble with boss...23

Change in work hours or conditions....................20

Change in residence..20

Change in school or college................................20

Change in recreation..19

Change in church activities................................19

Change in social activities.................................18

A moderate loan or mortgage...........................17

Change in sleeping habits................................16

Change in number of family get-togethers.......15

Change in eating habits..................................15

Holiday...13

Christmas..12

Minor violation of the law.............................11

The biological basis of stress

Our bodies react when they experience stress, whether the stress is caused by an emergency or a slow build-up of many changes. One of the main ways they do this is by the fight/flight reaction. This is the mechanism by which your body prepares to save itself from an enemy by either running away or standing and fighting. Some researchers believe that this reaction was evolved by early humans as a survival mechanism. It enables the body to use extra energy reserves and primes your heart and lungs for a burst of action.

When an emergency occurs, your hypothalamus (in your brain) secretes a special hormone (chemical messenger) called corticotrophin releasing factor. This hormone tells your pituitary gland (also in your brain) to secrete another hormone called adreno corticotrophin hormone, or ACTH. This hormone travels to your adrenal glands, which sit on top of your kidneys, and tells them to produce three more hormones: adrenalin, noradrenalin and cortisol. It sounds as if the reaction should take a long time, but in fact it is

Emergency

In an emergency, hormones race around your body, preparing it for action.

almost instantaneous. It needs to be. If you were a caveman suddenly coming face to face with a sabre tooth tiger you would want to be able to move fast!

The three hormones produced by your adrenal glands are the messengers that tell your body what to do.

- **Adrenalin** (also known as epinephrine) and **noradrenalin** (norepinephrine) have the effect of making your heart thump loudly in your chest whilst your skin goes pale and clammy. This means there is lots of blood available to deliver oxygen to your muscles and gives you an instant energy boost.

- **Noradrenalin** is also a neurotransmitter (a chemical that helps nerve cells communicate with each other) and it helps regulate your energy levels. It helps you get up in the morning and sleep at night.

- **Cortisol** helps protect your body from stress. It is involved in making sure that you have enough energy available to cope with an emergency situation and it acts as an anti-inflammatory agent (stopping swelling and redness) which helps the healing process.

The fight/flight reaction works well under normal conditions, but if you experience too much stress over a long period of time problems can occur. A high level of adrenalin over a long period can put you at risk of heart disease. Persistently high levels of cortisol can reduce the production of another important chemical called serotonin. This can lead to problems with your immune system, which can mean you get more coughs and colds. Serotonin also influences sleep patterns, which is why too much stress can lead to problems sleeping.

In this chapter we have investigated what happens when we experience too much stress. Next we will look at different ways to manage stress and prevent problems occurring.

3 Managing stress
Techniques to help you cope

In chapter 2 we looked at what happens when you are stressed. The list of problems that can result from too much stress is enormous. Sometimes, no matter how careful you are to keep healthy and manage stress, things can get too much. If this happens it is important to get help. Go and see your family doctor or other health professional and ask their advice. However, it saves a lot of boring time being ill if you can prevent stress becoming a problem in the first place. The good news is that there are many simple things that you can do to manage the stress in your life. We will look at these in this chapter.

Healthy eating

Being fit and healthy is a sure way to maximize your ability to manage stress. As we saw on page 19, being ill or unfit can reduce your ability to withstand stress. Healthy eating is vital to staying fit and healthy. A healthy diet includes:

- plenty of fresh fruit and vegetables
- lots of complex carbohydrates, such as wholemeal bread, potatoes, pasta and rice
- moderate amounts of protein-rich foods, such as fish, chicken, soya, nuts, pulses (beans), eggs or red meat
- fat, as in butter, margarine, oil, milk, and cheese, but in much smaller amounts.

Eating five servings of fruit or vegetables per day is recommended, to ensure an adequate daily vitamin intake. Vitamins are important as they help our bodies grow and function properly and fight off infections.

What you eat now will affect your health, and therefore the amount of stress in your life, as you grow older. Teenagers who eat too little calcium – present in milk, cheese, bread and green leafy vegetables – increase their risk of osteoporosis (brittle bones) as adults. Eating too much saturated fat when you are young can increase your risk of heart disease later in life.

As with most things in life, healthy eating involves moderation. Too much food or too little will cause your body chemistry to change and will therefore be a source of stress. If you feel that you weigh too much or too little, then talk to a doctor or health professional who will be able to give you an unbiased opinion and safe advice about changing your eating habits.

Watch your diet
A healthy diet consists of 35 per cent fruit and vegetables, 40 per cent complex carbohydrates, 20 per cent protein-rich food, and 5 per cent fat.

Exercise

Exercise is a vital part of fitness. The fitter you are, the better able you will be to manage the stresses of life. Exercise is also an excellent way to relax and 'turn off' for a while. Most experts feel that you need to do 20 to 30 minutes of exercise three times a week to stay healthy. However, if you have a health problem or if you are very unfit, it is best to consult your doctor before you start a new exercise programme.

It is important to find a form of exercise that you enjoy. Otherwise it can easily become boring. Some people find it better to incorporate exercise into their daily lives rather than going to special exercise classes. This can involve activities such as brisk walking or bicycling rather than taking the car or bus, and using the stairs rather than the lift. Whatever you do, start gradually and build up slowly.

Exercise class
Exercising together can be fun.

'I love my dancing classes. When I've been dancing, my heart sings and I feel I can tackle anything.'
(Amy, dance student)

Rest and relaxation

Learning to relax properly is a very good way of managing stress. It can help to reduce anxiety and combat the physical effects of too much stress such as chest pain and sleep problems. There are many different ways of relaxing. Some forms of exercise, such as swimming, are very good at leaving your body relaxed. Massage and hydrotherapy have a similar effect.

It is a good idea to learn a relaxation technique that you can use at times when you feel tense. It will calm you down, help you to clear your mind and think more clearly. There are many different relaxation techniques. One example is given on the right.

Relaxation technique

1 *Curl up your toes and tense your left foot. Let your foot relax. Think about it feeling warm and heavy and floppy. Repeat this twice.*

2 *Tense your left calf muscle and let it relax again. Think about your calf feeling warm and heavy and floppy. Repeat this twice.*

3 *Repeat this procedure with your left thigh, then with your right foot, calf and thigh.*

4 *Now move slowly up your body, tensing and relaxing and thinking about each individual area – your bottom, stomach, back, chest, right shoulder, left shoulder, right hand, right forearm, right upper arm, then your left arm, forearm and upper arm. Then slowly tense and relax your neck, then your jaw. Screw up your face and let it relax a few times.*

5 *Now you are fully relaxed, think about your breathing. Try to empty your mind of everything except breathing in and out. If other thoughts intrude, notice them, then put them away and think about your breathing again. Breathe slowly in through your nose, then out through your mouth. Repeat this for a few minutes as long as it feels comfortable.*

6 *Relax, and return to your normal activities.*

Tai chi
Tai chi is a Chinese system of exercise and self-defence, which also helps people feel calmer and relaxed.

Avoiding harmful substances

All drugs, including prescribed drugs, caffeine, alcohol, nicotine (from cigarettes) and illegal drugs, cause changes to your body chemistry and therefore stress. Drugs prescribed for you by a doctor, and taken as directed by the doctor or pharmacist, can help you to become healthier. Healthy people manage stress a lot better than unhealthy people.

Taking any drug *without* medical necessity will increase the level of stress you have to deal with. This is true even for drugs like caffeine, which is found in tea and coffee. If you drink too much strong coffee your heart will race, you may feel shaky and get a headache. Caffeine changes the chemistry of your body and you have to work hard to restore things to normal. Other drugs act in different ways, but all of them change your body chemistry, some to such an extent that you can become addicted to them.

Taking illegal drugs or even legal ones like alcohol can cause stressful problems on a much wider scale than just the chemical changes in your body. Violence is far more likely in situations that involve alcohol. Arguments, social problems, financial problems and criminal prosecutions are all more common for people who abuse drugs.

Party pressure
Is it more difficult to resist pressure to take drugs in the atmosphere of a party or night club?

The best way to manage this kind of stress is to avoid unnecessary drugs. It can be hard to resist pressure from other people to try drugs and there are many programmes that can help you work out effective ways to say no. It is wise to make sure that you are well informed about the good and bad effects of all drugs. If you do decide to take illegal drugs make sure you know what the penalties are if you are caught by the police. What will be the effect on your family, friends, work and school?

If you have an addiction problem it is important to seek help. Many organizations exist to help people fight addiction. Your family doctor or local health clinic will be able to give you information on what is available in your area.

Kicking the habit

I've been off the ciggies about 3 months now. It wasn't as hard as I've heard it is. I'd been smoking for about two years, on and off. I started because everyone did it, all my friends – well, nearly all. They said it helped you get thin and calm down and things. It was OK at first. Just the odd one on the way home from school. Then it got more. If things got on top of me, I had to have a cigarette to get me through. But they didn't calm me down. They hyped me up really – shaky hands and things. Then Mum found out and all hell broke loose ... going on about the smell, and the stains on my fingers and the cost. So I stopped. I was worried I was going to get fat but I didn't. My breathing improved really quickly so I could run for the bus.
(Kayleigh, 15 years old)

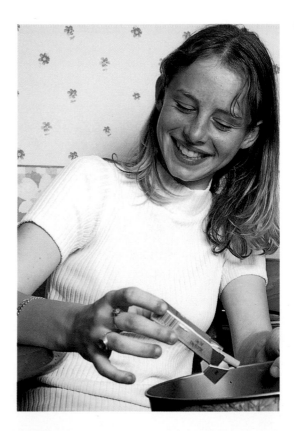

Problem solving

Problem solving is a useful strategy for managing stressful situations. It can help you stand back from a situation and get a better sense of perspective about it. The idea behind problem solving is that you approach a problem in a logical and systematic fashion.

How to problem solve

1   Sit down with a piece of paper and work out exactly what the problem is. You may find that there is more than one problem, or that some of your problems are really worries. Make a list of your problems.

2   Make a list of different ways of dealing with each problem. Brainstorm: write down anything you can think of that might help the situation.

3   Think carefully about the different strategies you have come up with: what would happen if you tried each one? Pick a strategy that you think will be safe and effective. It can be helpful to talk through the options with a friend. Make sure you think about how your strategy will affect other people.

4   Try out the strategy.

5   Evaluate how effective it was. Did it work? Did it help a bit? How can you improve on the strategy?

Thinking
Writing problems down can help you to think about ways to solve them.

The problem of the suspect package

David is worried. Simon has asked him to look after a parcel overnight, as he doesn't want it at home. David felt really pleased to be asked, as Simon is very popular, but now he isn't so sure. David's best friend thinks the parcel might have drugs in it. If it has, and the police find it at David's house, both David and his parents could be in big trouble. The problem is what to do with the parcel. David could:

What would you do?

a. throw it in the bin and pretend to Simon that he lost it
b. open it
c. tell his parents about it
d. take it home and risk it
e. hide it somewhere away from home and give it back to Simon the next day as arranged
f. take it back to Simon straight away and risk the ridicule.

David rejects options a, b and c as being out of the question. This leaves him with options d, e and f. In the end he decides to hide the parcel and take it back to Simon tomorrow as he can't put his parents at risk and he doesn't want to risk the taunts if he takes it straight back. But he swears never to do it again. What would you do?

Social situations

Social situations, such as talking to friends or acquaintances, teachers or colleagues, can be stressful. There are many rules in society about the way we talk and act with each other and it can be very difficult to learn them. Unfortunately, 'How to win friends and influence people' is not usually a subject option at school.

One way to improve your social skills is to join a drama group. Drama teaches you to imagine what it is like to be someone else. Being able to imagine how another person is feeling is a very important skill to learn. It helps you to be sensitive to other people's needs and interested in their lives (especially important when making friends or chatting up girls). Drama can also help you overcome difficult feelings such as shyness. Pretending or acting being happy and confident can help you to actually become happy and confident.

Drama
Acting can help you learn how to communicate with others.

Role-play

Role-play involves imagining a situation – for example, how to resist friends trying to get you to smoke – and then working through how you could manage it. What could you say? How might people react? Other people can have helpful ideas on different ways to say or do things, so it is best to do role-play with a good friend or two, but pick your partners carefully and think through all your ideas thoroughly. That way, any stupid or dangerous ideas can be weeded out whilst you are practising.

Assertiveness

Assertiveness is an important skill that can help you to manage stress. When you are being assertive, you stand up for yourself and express your point of view in a manner that is direct, honest, appropriate to your situation, and respectful of the needs of the people you are dealing with. In order to become assertive you need to practise again with role-play. This is best done in a group or with good friends, as you really need other people to help you decide what is assertive, what is meek and what is aggressive.

Being a friend

Everyone experiences too much stress at some time. This means that the people you live and work with, your friends and family, colleagues and teachers are all just as likely to be suffering from too much stress as you are. Remember that everyone's ability to manage stress depends to a certain extent on the people around them. Good friends and a loving family help a person to manage stress.

'Acting has really helped me overcome my shyness. I still feel shy sometimes, but I know how to act as if I'm not. Sometimes I even fool myself.' (Alan, actor)

We all need to help each other to manage stress. There are various ways you can do this. The most obvious way is by listening. It is a common saying that a problem shared is a problem halved, but it is not just problems we have to listen to. In order to have healthy, supportive relationships, you need to be able to share joys and sorrows. Listening is a skill that can be learnt. It is very easy to get into the habit of not listening to people properly. Listening involves being active. Pay attention to what people say and what they don't say, the things they half say, or begin to say and then change the subject. Often these are as important as what is actually said. Sometimes it is easier for people to talk about things if they are doing something else. Lots of good chats occur whilst washing up or cooking. Being supportive involves making time for people, listening and caring about what they are saying.

Often, when people experience too much stress, they feel low and negative. It can help them to know that you love and value them. Tell them the things that you like about them. You don't have to be gushy about this, just honest and positive. If someone does something you like or admire, tell them. Even brothers and sisters need cheering up sometimes.

In this chapter we have looked at different ways of managing stress. In the next chapter we will be looking at a condition that can result from too much stress, depression.

Good friends
Having good friends can help you to manage stress.

CHAPTER 3

Walking Dad

Last summer Dad started acting strange. I don't mean he started doing funny walks or anything, just not normal. They started making people redundant in his office and I suppose he was worried that he'd be next. Then my sister got in with a bad crowd at school and started coming in late. He went ballistic, red in the face and everything. Then Gran got ill and I suppose he was worrying about her too. He started drinking more. He had problems sleeping, he looked permanently tired and kept getting ill – colds and things.

I didn't know what to do. It was worrying Mum, too. Then I had an idea. I got this leaflet from the doctors on fitness and started talking to him about it. I said I wanted to get fit but I couldn't do it on my own and would he help me? Well, he fell for it, and we decided to go for a jog every night together. It was more of a fast walk at first really, but it worked. If he wasn't sitting in front of the telly he didn't drink so much and he slept a lot better with the exercise. Actually, so did I. It didn't get rid of all his problems, but it sure helped us all deal with them. Apart from my sister that is. She still gets in late.

(Jo, 17 years old)

4 What is depression?
Symptoms and causes

Depression, like stress, is a word we hear nearly every day. People talk about feeling depressed if they are a bit low, or they will say that the weather is depressing if it is raining. Sometimes you hear people saying that they are depressed because they are having a bad hair day or because their favourite team lost a game. People talk about things that make them feel sad or low as depressing. These feelings usually improve over a few hours or days.

A bad hair day
Depression is worse than feeling down on a 'bad hair day'.

The medical term 'depression' refers to an illness in which people feel very sad and low for several weeks or months. People who have depression often have no energy and feel tired all the time. They lose their enthusiasm for life and seem to get no enjoyment even from their favourite pastimes. Depressed people can lose their appetite and may lose weight. They often sleep badly and the sadness can seem worse in the morning. They may have trouble concentrating and taking in information, and this can make working difficult. Sometimes people who are depressed feel so bad that they feel they would be better off dead.

Depression is a particularly nasty illness that affects about one in five people during their lifetime. Depression can be a moderate or a severe illness. About one in ten people will experience an episode of severe depression. The good news is that depression is treatable. Modern medicines and therapies are very effective at treating depression.

Depression and young people

It is only relatively recently (over the last ten years or so) that the medical profession has begun to recognize depression in young people. Before this time, it was thought that young people felt sad and unhappy for a long time as a result of puberty. However, now, it is recognized that young people do suffer from depression, though it is less common than in adults. It has been estimated that about 1 per cent of children under the age of 12 and about 3 per cent of young people between the ages of 12 and 16 will experience an episode of severe depression.

A treatable illness

Depression is a treatable illness. You just have to ask for help.

Hanna and the black box

Hi, my name is Hanna, and I have depression. I don't like telling people that I have depression. I worry that people will think I'm mad. I'm not mad, just very sad, and I have been for a long time. What does being depressed feel like? Well, it is very hard to describe. It goes up and down. When it is bad, it feels a bit like sitting inside a big black box when everyone else is on the outside. You can't feel them or talk to them and they can't hear or touch you. There is just blackness and no way out. I can't cope with people talking to me. I find it hard to concentrate on what they are saying. They talk too quickly. My Mum is brilliant. She had depression once and understands. She sits and holds my hand and talks to me quietly and slowly. My doctor says it is an illness, like arthritis or diabetes, and that it can be cured with treatment. I hope so. I know in my head that I will get better, but my heart doesn't believe it yet. Mum says just hold on. The tablets will work soon. So I'm holding on and trying to hope.
(Hanna is 17 years old.)

Depression in adults and young people is very similar. In both groups, the person experiences persistent sadness, loss of concentration and loss of appetite. They may also have problems sleeping and lose their enthusiasm for life. However, there are some differences. Young people with depression can be more irritable than adults. They are more likely to have learning and behaviour problems. Depressed young people may truant from school and they often have other symptoms such as headaches or stomach aches. These things can make it more difficult for doctors to recognize depression in young people. But once it is identified it is treatable and can be cured.

Irritability
When young people become depressed they are often very irritable.

Depression around the world
According to the World Health Organization in 1990 depression was the leading cause of disease worldwide, accounting for 10 per cent of all disease, deaths and disability around the world.

Top of the league

This graph shows the main causes of disease worldwide, and the percentages of the total burden of disease and disability they account for.

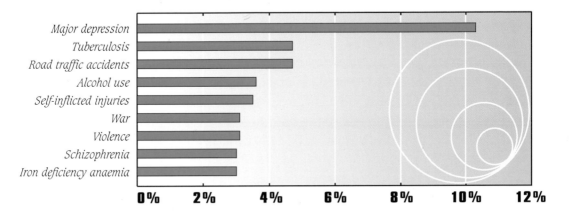

Depression is a common illness across the whole world. However, there are some cultural differences in the way people experience depression. For example, in India, people tend to report more physical symptoms of depression, especially symptoms like 'burning skin' or 'fire inside'.

Some people estimate that depression rates are as much as 50 per cent lower in the Far East (countries like China and Taiwan) than in the West. This may be due to the culture of close family ties in such countries. Close family support may be protective against depression, but there is an increased incidence of anxiety-related problems in these countries which may be a result of stress from family relations.

Anxiety

Anxiety is a normal response to a threatening situation. It prepares you to deal with danger. Feeling anxious involves having an unpleasant feeling that something bad is going to happen.

Sometimes people experience so much anxiety that it causes anxiety-related problems including:

- *finding it difficult to be with people*
- *being over-sensitive to criticism*
- *worrying excessively about events*
- *finding it difficult to stop worrying*
- *disturbed sleep*
- *poor concentration*
- *tiredness.*

The causes of depression

Many people who have experienced depression report that they felt as if a switch had been turned off in their brain. It is true that there are chemical changes in the brains of depressed people, and we will investigate these in the next chapter. What causes or triggers these chemical changes depends on the individual.

You are more likely to suffer from depression at some time during your life if you have a close relative who has suffered from depression. You are twice as likely to experience depression if you are a woman. This is true all over the world and may be due to several factors. First, women tend to be poorer and have less control over their circumstances than men. Poverty, loneliness and low social status can all contribute to depression. But the main reason women are more at risk from depression is probably to do with hormones.

The hormone oestrogen, which is part of the female menstrual cycle, is known to help protect against depression. However, the level of this hormone goes up and down during a woman's monthly cycle. Women often feel quite low when the levels of oestrogen drop just before their periods. This is known as the pre-menstrual phase. Women are also prone to depression at other times when oestrogen is at a low level, such as after the birth of a baby (post-natal depression) and at menopause (when a woman's periods stop as she gets older).

Men have a lower level of oestrogen in their bodies than women, but this level does not

A woman's life?
Traditionally, a woman's role in family life has increased her risk of stress and depression.

change. As we discussed in Chapter 1, any change is stressful and therefore the constant state of hormonal change for women may make them more vulnerable to depression.

Too much stress can trigger depression, as can alcohol or drug use. The time of year can also affect people. Seasonal affective disorder (SAD) is the name given to a depressive illness that some people get during winter. It is more common in the Northern Hemisphere and it seems to be related to day length. So, for some people, as the days get shorter, their symptoms of depression get worse and as the days lengthen in spring, they start to feel better.

Extra light
This girl who suffers from SAD has a light box to supplement the winter daylight.

Events such as the death of a loved one are often linked to depression, as are child abuse, bullying and sexuality issues. Worrying about being homosexual is a common cause of depression in young men. Below is a list of common triggers of depression. In the next chapter we will look at what happens when you are depressed, the biological basis of depression and its consequences.

Common triggers of depression

Moving house	*Serious injury or illness of a loved one*
Divorce or separation	*Money worries*
Death of a loved one	*Unemployment*
Long-term alcohol or drug use	*Winter*
Certain medicines	*Loneliness*
Problems at work	*Problems with a spouse or partner*
Long-term physical illness	*Childbirth*
Low self-esteem	*Menopause*
Being a victim of a crime or an accident	*Too much stress*

5 What happens when you are depressed?
A chemical imbalance

When you have depression several things happen. First, for sad feelings to be classified as an illness rather than just the normal ups and downs of life, you have to have been feeling unhappy for more than two weeks. Other signs of depression include:

Life's ups and downs

Depression involves feeling sad for more than two weeks.

- feeling low for most of the day (especially in the morning)
- decreased amount of pleasure or interest in life
- weight loss or gain
- sleeping too much or too little
- reduced control over bodily movements
- tiredness
- feeling worthless and guilty
- difficulty concentrating
- hopelessness

- low self-esteem
- thinking about death or suicide
- anxiety
- difficulty in relationships with other people
- lowered libido (sex drive).

People who are grieving after the death of a loved one often experience the symptoms of depression. However they do not usually require medical treatment unless they do not feel better after several months.

Young people with depression may experience all these symptoms plus some others. They tend to be more irritable and also experience more vague physical symptoms such as headaches and stomach aches. They may also express their depression slightly differently, tending to display more behaviour problems, anger and sometimes self-harm.

Not hungry
Loss of appetite is one symptom of depression.

Self-harm

Self-harm means damaging yourself on purpose, for instance by cutting, using scissors, knives, razors or pins, poisoning or suffocation. Self-harm can result in suicide, even if it was not intended. Reasons people give for harming themselves include:

- *stress*
- *anxiety*
- *depression*
- *poor self-esteem*
- *lack of confidence*
- *attention-seeking*
- *revenge*
- *punishment.*

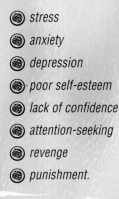

All the symptoms and feelings of depression happen because of chemical changes in the brain.

Nerve to nerve

In your brain, messages are transmitted from one nerve cell to another. The chemical messengers must jump across the tiny gap between cells (detail a). If the messengers are not working normally, you may feel low or depressed.

(a)

The biological basis of depression

There are approximately one million million nerve cells within the human brain. Nerve cells communicate with each other via chemical messengers. Each cell receives a mixture of chemical messages that excite or inhibit it to varying extents. Under normal conditions the chemical messengers are in balance, the nerve cells communicate properly and your brain functions normally.

When you experience too much stress or a trigger event, problems can begin to occur. As your brain experiences more stress, the levels of exciting chemical messengers may begin to drop. This means that the nerve cells in your brain become less active and more sluggish. This prevents them operating properly and can result in you beginning to develop the symptoms of depression. As your brain cells become less active and the chemical messenger levels drop, you feel low and miserable. Normally your brain is able to right this imbalance over a short period of time but if it continues for a long time you may go on to develop depression.

There are three main chemical messengers that stop working properly when you are depressed. These are serotonin, noradrenalin (norepinephrine) and dopamine.

Serotonin

Serotonin helps your body get ready for sleep and plays a big part in setting your body clock. Your body clock is a very important mechanism that keeps your body functioning in rhythm. It controls your body temperature, lowering it at night and raising it in the morning to ensure you have the energy to get out of bed and face the day. It also controls your sleep cycles, helping to make you feel tired in the evening and have the right amount of deep sleep and dream sleep to refresh and renew you. It is also involved in the production of a hormone called cortisol.

Cortisol is a hormone that helps your body fight stress. If your cortisol levels are high, then your body is ready to

Sleep

A normal night's sleep can be divided into quiet sleep and active (dreaming) sleep. These follow each other in regular cycles while you are asleep.

Quiet sleep is made up of four stages ranging from stage 1 – dozing to stage 4 – deep sleep. It is during deep sleep that your body is most active, repairing, healing and growing.

Active (dreaming) sleep is sometimes called REM (rapid eye movement) sleep. It is during this phase of sleep that you dream. Adults usually dream for a total of about an hour and a half each night. Most dreams are forgotten as soon as you awake.

run or fight. If your body clock is working properly, the levels of cortisol in your body will drop in the evening. This helps you to relax and prepares you for a restful night's sleep. If the levels of cortisol do not drop in the evening, which can happen if you experience too much stress, you will find it hard to get off to sleep.

So, serotonin helps control your body clock and your body clock controls your body temperature, your deep sleep and dreaming cycles and the levels of cortisol. If the levels of serotonin in your body are low, the rhythm of your daily life will be disrupted and it can be very difficult to get a good night's sleep.

Refreshed

When your body clock (controlled by serotonin) is working well, you wake up feeling full of energy and ready to start the day.

Noradrenalin (norepinephrine)

Noradrenalin is one of the hormones that are produced when you have a shock. It is related to the hormone adrenalin that makes your heartbeat faster and your skin pale and clammy. Noradrenalin is also a chemical messenger in your

brain. It is involved in setting your energy levels, and helps you to feel full of energy and enthusiasm. If you are depressed, then your levels of noradrenalin may be low, and you will feel lifeless and exhausted. Your level of enthusiasm will be low even for things you usually love.

Dopamine

Dopamine plays an important role in how we experience pleasure. If the production of this messenger is decreased then it is hard to feel pleased about anything. Dopamine production is also associated with the production of a group of chemicals called endorphins. Endorphins are a form of painkiller that is found naturally in our brains. If the level of dopamine in our brain decreases, the level of endorphins also tends to drop. Therefore, for people who have severe depression where the production of these two chemicals is greatly reduced, life can become very painful and without pleasure.

Enjoying a laugh
Dopamine controls our ability to experience pleasure.

Suicide

Depression is a serious illness and can be fatal. Being depressed is a distressing experience and sometimes people who are suffering from it feel so hopeless and worthless that they think they would rather be dead. It has been estimated that between 10 and 15 per cent of depressed adults will succeed in killing themselves and nearly 30 per cent will attempt it. Suicide rates tend to be higher for men and older people. They also tend to be higher for those who are bereaved or separated. Married people have a much lower risk of suicide.

Certain jobs and professions have a high suicide rate. These include doctors, lawyers, hotel workers, nurses and writers. However depression is not the only illness that can result in suicide. Other conditions that are associated with suicide include schizophrenia, alcoholism and drug abuse. As many as 25 per cent of alcoholics and drug addicts take their own life.

Suicide among adolescents is still relatively uncommon, despite the coverage it gets in the news. However, it is still the second most common cause of death in adolescents after accidents. During the 1990s the number of young people, particularly young men, taking their own life

Feeling too bad to go on
Between 10 and 15 per cent of depressed adults commit suicide.

increased, but now the rate seems to be declining again. Why this happened is hard to say, although some people think that it may have been due to men rethinking their role in modern society.

Many depressed people have suicidal thoughts, and it is estimated that as many as 50 per cent of healthy adolescents will have suicidal thoughts every week. To *think* about committing suicide is common, but that is a long way from actually doing it. Young people tend to display two types of suicide attempts, deliberate suicide and self-harm. Of those young people who succeed in killing themselves, about half are affected by alcohol or drug abuse. For the remainder, suicide seems to be associated with a sense of hopelessness. Suicide attempts can also be a means of expressing anger or hostility, of making someone else feel guilty, or of gaining attention. Self-harm is a complex issue associated with self-esteem, self-confidence, worries, anxiety and depression.

Of the people who successfully commit suicide, about 60 per cent have told someone of their intention. People who say they feel suicidal should never be ignored. Always take talk of suicide seriously. Someone who is feeling desperate enough to think about taking their own life needs love, support and professional medical care.

If someone says they feel suicidal ...

1 *Always take talk of suicide seriously. The idea that people who talk of suicide won't do it is not true.*

2 *Try to discuss the person's feelings gently and kindly.*

3 *Ask them to tell someone else – a parent, teacher, friend – and see their doctor.*

4 *If they will not talk to anyone else then you need to tell someone, even if you have been asked not to. This is a situation where betraying a confidence to a responsible person is justified.*

Looking after Mum

My Mum's depressed, had it for ages – at least, it seems like ages. Dad says we're not to tell anyone, because they'll think we're all a bit soft in the head. Mum just sits there and doesn't say anything. She stares at her hands and cries quietly. Sometimes I sit with her and hold her hand. I think she likes it. She tries to smile. She says she's sorry and we deserve better than her and that's really hard because there's no one better than her. Gran says she's lazy and needs to get off her backside and cook us a decent meal. I don't think she's lazy, she's ill.

Standing in

Young people like Katy may need to stand in for their depressed parent for their younger siblings.

So I tell Gran to shut up and then we have a row about me being rude. I worry about Mum all the time. I worry when I come back to the house in case, you know, in case she's done something stupid.

There's this chap who comes to see us about Mum, a nurse I think. He says she will get better but it will take time. I wish it would go away right now.
(Katy, 15 years old)

Living with people who are depressed

People with depression often find it hard to tell others what is wrong with them. They fear that other people will think they are mad. They worry that, if people know they have had depression once, they will consider them weak forever. This is not true. Most people who become ill with depression will not have it again. Depression is an awful experience and people who have suffered from it are often much stronger afterwards and better able to stand up to the trials of life. Some people do go on to suffer from depression periodically throughout their lives, but this is not very common.

Being with a person who is depressed can be exhausting. People who are depressed find it hard to communicate and are very sensitive to criticism. The sun may be shining and everything may seem fine to you, but a depressed person will see nothing but gloom and disaster. They may be irritable, and young depressed people may be hostile and aggressive. Family and friends need to be supportive not only to the person who is depressed but to each other as well.

'Since I had depression, I've re-evaluated my life. If something's not important I don't let it bother me. Life is too precious to worry about things that don't matter.'
(John, company director)

The strain of living with a depressed person can cause irritability and stress-related problems for other family members. Unfortunately, there are still people who do not understand that depression is a medical illness. They may feel that the depressed person just needs to 'pull themselves together' or 'snap out of it'. People who say these things may mean well, but their lack of understanding can make things worse. This sort of attitude can also put additional strain on the families of people who are depressed, leaving them feeling isolated.

In the next chapter we will look at different treatments for depression and practical ways in which you can support someone who is depressed.

6 Beating depression
The range of treatments

Depression is a common medical problem and can be treated. Your family doctor or a psychiatrist is responsible for providing appropriate treatment. Psychiatrists are doctors who specialize in treating disorders or illnesses of the mind. People with depression often experience severe mental anguish and psychiatrists specialize in helping them.

Depression can be treated by a variety of therapies. These can be prescribed singly or as a mixture. Which therapy works best depends on the individual, so if one method doesn't help there are other options.

Drug therapy

Drug therapy is a common treatment for depression. The drugs used are known as antidepressants and they are not addictive. They work by regulating the build-up of neurotransmitters (chemicals that affect the brain and nervous system), such as serotonin and noradrenalin in nerve endings.

It can take two to three weeks for the medicine to reach high enough levels in your brain. This means that it can seem a long time before any improvement is felt. Antidepressants are very effective. Sixty to seventy per cent of people who take antidepressants will recover in six to eight weeks. However, it can be difficult for depressed people to keep taking medication for a long time without any noticeable improvement, and they may also experience side effects.

The side effects of antidepressants vary depending on which type is prescribed (there are over 30 varieties). Some types have a much lower risk of side effects. Common side effects include blurred vision, dry mouth, constipation, nausea and headaches.

Antidepressants are not addictive, but they usually need to be taken for at least three months after the depression has lifted and then the dose is reduced slowly. This is to make sure that the depression doesn't return. Some types of antidepressants work better with young people than others. Some react with other medicines. Doctors need to take all these things into account when prescribing them.

The baby blues
Postnatal depression can affect one in ten women.

Turning the baby blues rosy pink

Jane gave birth to a beautiful baby girl three months ago. After the birth she found life very hard. She felt a failure and unable to cope with looking after the baby. She was tired, cried a lot and despaired that she would ever get better. Last month Jane's doctor diagnosed her as suffering from postnatal depression. She prescribed Jane an antidepressant that would not affect her ability to breast-feed and Jane's partner took some time off work to help her. Jane is beginning to feel better now. She still has bad days, but she is sleeping better and some days now she doesn't cry at all. Best of all, today, the baby smiled at her.

Talking therapy

Another group of treatments for depression that can be very effective are called talking therapies or psychotherapies. There are many different types of talking therapies. We will look at the most common: counselling, cognitive therapy and family therapy.

Counselling

Counselling is used as a treatment for many different conditions including depression. It usually involves going to see a trained psychologist or counsellor weekly or monthly for a period of time. The counsellor helps you to explore what may have triggered the depression, events in the past that might have contributed to it and ways of managing your feelings in the future. Everything you say during a counselling session is kept completely confidential.

Counsellors look at every person they see as an individual with unique problems. They help their clients overcome anxiety, fear and other strong emotions by reliving them during the counselling session, in a safe environment.

Therapy

For some people, counselling and cognitive therapy can be as effective as antidepressants in treating depression.

They help each individual to understand how he or she reacts to others and to rehearse better ways of managing relationships.

Counsellors also try to help their clients improve their self-knowledge. This involves trying to work out why we respond to events in certain ways. The idea is that, once you understand why you act in a certain way, then you can change it. Counselling is a gradual process and a good counsellor will take clients step by step through the process of understanding what their problems are and why and help them to manage and overcome these problems. The effectiveness of counselling in treating depression varies but usually it is helpful for about 30 per cent of people.

Cognitive therapy

Cognitive therapy is based on the idea that negative or sad thoughts are not just the *result* of depression but also play a part in *causing* depression. The aim of cognitive therapy is to change the way an individual thinks, in order to change the way they behave and feel. The idea is that depression is caused by the way we have learnt to deal with problems, and that it can be treated by learning new ways to manage sad thoughts.

'Cognitive therapy needs commitment. It's a long process, but the transformation in a person's life can be astounding. It's very rewarding.'
(Anna, cognitive therapist)

Cognitive therapy usually involves going to see a trained therapist for about 20 sessions over three or four months. During therapy you are taught to recognize the sad thoughts that accompany depression. You then set goals and learn different techniques for achieving those goals. Typical goals might be getting up at a specific time in the morning, or going for a walk. People with depression can find what seem simple things very hard. Techniques for achieving goals include:

 examining sad thoughts to see if things are really as bad as they feel

 relaxation techniques

⚫ role-play

⚫ problem solving.

The aim is to move from being unaware of sad thoughts to being aware of them. Then the sad thoughts gradually become less upsetting until they are overcome. Cognitive therapy is very effective at treating depression. It seems to be as effective as antidepressant drugs for people with mild to moderate depression.

Family therapy

Family therapy is a form of talking therapy for the whole family. The aim is to try to establish how relationships within the family work. Issues can be talked through in a safe environment, and different ways of being together explored. Family therapy is most commonly used for young people with depression. It can help open up channels of communication and improve supportive relationships within the family. Family therapy usually complements other treatments such as antidepressants.

Digging the bogeyman out of the wardrobe

Family therapy has been really excellent. It's dug the bogeyman out of the wardrobe in my head. I'd been depressed for weeks – I mean really bad. Couldn't get up, couldn't face school. Anna, my therapist, sees all of us, Mum, Dad and my brother. I didn't realize I was so hung up about Mum and Dad rowing. I thought it was my fault, but it wasn't, just money stuff. I mean, that's bad, but at least it's not me. That's why they haven't been listening – too busy with their own worries. Well, at least they have to listen to me in therapy. They're trying at home, too. Things are much better.
(Holly, aged 15)

Hospitalization

People with depression are not usually admitted to hospital. They can be treated effectively at home. However, for some people who are at grave risk of suicide and have severe depression, a stay in hospital can be helpful. Some people feel safer in hospital where they are looked after and closely supervised. Patients usually stay only a short time while they are severely ill. Then they are sent home and helped to start living a normal life again.

Electro-convulsive therapy (ECT)

Electro-convulsive therapy is only used to treat the most severe cases of depression where the person has not responded to normal treatments and is at grave risk of committing suicide. They have usually experienced severe depressions over many years and are desperately in need of help. For these people ECT can be a lifesaver, and the symptoms of depression relieved very quickly.

Having ECT involves visiting a hospital or clinic. The patient is given an anaesthetic and then a small amount of electric current is passed across their brain for two to three seconds. This causes an artificial epileptic fit whilst the patient is asleep and unaware of what is happening.

It is the fit, rather than the electricity, that helps change the levels of neurotransmitters in the brain back to normal. ECT can cause side effects. Sometimes people experience memory loss of recent events, or of names and telephone numbers. Usually this gets better within a few days or weeks, but for some people it takes longer.

ECT has a bad reputation because many years ago some people who lived in psychiatric institutions were given ECT against their will. These days the use of ECT is regulated. There are laws about patient consent that prevent people being given unwanted treatment, except in carefully controlled circumstances. ECT is very effective with severe depression in 8 out of 10 people.

Overcoming depression

There are several things you can do to help yourself fight depression:

- Don't be afraid to ask for help. Depression is a serious illness and requires medical treatment.
- Take medication as prescribed by your doctor.
- Talk to people; don't bottle things up. Share your feelings with close family and friends.
- Try to keep active. Take some exercise – for example, go for a long walk. This may help you to sleep better and can help distract you from sad thoughts.
- Eat a well-balanced diet, with lots of fruit and vegetables.
- Avoid drugs and alcohol as these can make the feelings worse.
- Don't worry if you can't sleep. Try to distract your mind by watching TV or listening to the radio as you rest your body.
- Remind yourself that you are suffering from an illness and that it will get better. Depression is very common. Lots of people suffer from it and you are not alone.
- It can be helpful to talk to other people who have experienced what you are going through. Your family doctor should be able to put you in touch with a suitable support group.
- If you feel suicidal, tell your doctor. They will be able to help you.

Helping others

There are some things you can do to help other people who are suffering from depression:

- Find out all you can about depression. People who are suffering from depression can find it very difficult to concentrate and remember new information. You can help by learning it for them and then reminding them when necessary that depression is a medical illness and they will get better.

- Be a good listener and a patient one. You may have to hear the same tale of woe again and again. This is part of the natural healing of the mind and can be very helpful for the sufferer.

- Spend time with them. Try to be relaxed and calm. If the person is very depressed, they will have trouble concentrating and following a conversation. Try not to talk too quickly, and concentrate on one subject at a time.

- Encourage the individual to keep going with at least part of their normal routine. Be gently positive with them about their achievements.

- Make sure that they are eating properly.

- Help them to stay away from alcohol and drugs.

- If they talk of suicide, take it seriously and make sure they keep their doctor informed.

- Help them to accept help and treatment.

- Look after yourself. Talk to a health professional yourself if you are worried. You will need support too. There are many groups that aim to help the families of people who are depressed. Don't be afraid to contact them. They are full of people going through the same problems you are.

Resources

Recommended reading

The following individual leaflets are a good introduction to the many aspects of depression. They are published by the Royal College of Psychiatrists, 17 Belgrave Square, London SW1X 8PG.

Help is at hand
Alcohol and depression
Anorexia and Bulimia
Anxiety and Phobias
Bereavement
Sleep problems
Depression in the elderly
Depression in the workplace
Depression in people with learning disability
Manic depression
Surviving adolescence
Men behaving sadly
Postnatal depression

Philip Graham and Carol Hughs, *So Young, so sad, so listen*, Gaskell, 1995
A book mainly for parents and teachers but with lots of useful information about depression in young people and how to support them.

Aidan Macfarlane and Ann McPherson, John Alstrop, *The New diary of a teenage health freak*, Oxford Paperbacks, 1996.
Funny, easy-to-read introduction to all health education issues including stress and depression.

Lewis Wolpert, *Malignant Sadness. The anatomy of depression*, Faber & Faber, 1999
A very useful serious book which clearly explains current theories about depression. Gives an excellent insight into what it is like to have depression.

Films

Most films are about stress and its impact on people. Very few deal specifically with depression, probably because it would be depressing to watch. The films listed here deal with depression and suicide from the safety of humour.

Life is Sweet, 1990, directed by Mike Leigh, is a film full of black humour and poignancy in which a family struggles to cope with a daughter who has bulimia and depression. It is particularly interesting for the way the family tries to adapt and develop new ways of communicating with each other.

Dead Poets Society, 1989, directed by Peter Wier, is about a group of boys growing up at boarding school and their new English teacher (Robin Williams). It focuses on the tensions between one boy's need to express himself and his father's expectations that ultimately lead to suicide.

Manhattan, 1979, written and directed by Woody Allen, is about the sex life of a writer who is obsessed by New York.

Woody Allen takes a humorous look at life, stress and anxiety that takes his central character close to despair and depression.

The Lonely Guy, 1984, directed by Arthur Hiller and starring Steve Martin, is a comedy in which a guy, thrown out by his girlfriend, sinks slowly into depression.

Cartoons
The Simpsons takes a sideways look at life in the USA, and has lots to say about the stresses of modern life and how we deal with them.

Websites
www.stress.org.uk
Directory of links relating to stress including information and therapists.

www.rcpsych.ac.uk
Royal College of Psychiatrists website. Lots of information about mental health topics plus many of the leaflets mentioned above available to download.

www.who.int/msa/mhn/ems/primacare/edukit/webdep.pdf
The World Health Organization's downloadable education kit on depression. Lots of easy-to-read information plus some self-help guidance.

www.teachhealth.com
Explains the medical basis of stress and depression in an easy-to-read format.

Sources used for this book
N. R. Carlson, *Physiology of behaviour*, 3rd edition, Allyn and Bacon Inc, 1986

S. G. Forman, *Coping skills, Interventions for Children and Adolescents*, Jossy-Bass publishers, San Francisco, 1993

R. J. Haggerty, L. R. Sherwood, N. Garmezy and M. Rutter, *Stress, Risk, and resilience in children and adolescents*, Cambridge University Press, 1966

Aidan Macfarlane and Ann McPherson, *Teenagers, the agony, the ecstasy, the answers*, Little, Brown & Company, 1999

Peter Makin, Cary Cooper, Charles Cox, *Managing people at work*, The British Psychological Society & Routledge Ltd, 1989

Lewis Wolpert, *Malignant Sadness. The anatomy of depression*, Faber & Faber, 1999

www.rcpsych.ac.uk (Royal College of Psychiatrists website)
www.who.int/msa/mhn/ems/primacare/edukit/wepdep.pdf (WHO's downloadable education kit on depression)
www.who.int/msa/mnh/ems/dalys/intro.htm: (WHO, Assessment of the changing global burden of disease from 1990 - 2020)

Glossary

anxiety the unpleasant feelings of apprehension and dread that you get when you are worrying about things. Anxiety can vary in severity from a mild feeling of uneasiness to panic attacks.

culture the way an individual society lives and works and plays, its rules and values. These tend to vary depending on geography, history and belief. There are many varied cultures, which look at the world in slightly different ways.

depression a medical illness that causes many problems. It is characterized by loss of interest in the pleasures of life and feelings of sadness for a long period of time.

diagnosis identification of the disease or illness that is causing a person problems.

endorphins pain-relieving chemicals that are produced naturally in the brain.

genetic We inherit characteristics from our parents via the genetic information that is present in every cell of our bodies. This information acts as a blueprint controlling how we grow, what colour our eyes and hair are and even things like whether we tend to have a short temper.

hormone Hormones are a group of chemical messengers produced by glands or organs in our bodies and which affect other parts of our bodies. The hormone adrenalin is produced by the adrenal glands and has an effect upon the heart, muscles, blood supply, skin and brain.

menopause the time during which a woman's periods gradually stop. It is a time of great hormonal change and adjustment.

menstruation the monthly discharge of blood and the lining of the uterus in women. Usually a sign that pregnancy has not occurred.

physical to do with the body or the way it works.

pre-menstrual to do with the time of hormonal change before menstruation.

psychological to do with the mind and behaviour.

puberty the time during which human males and females become physically mature and able to reproduce.

social to do with any situation involving two or more people, or with how people relate and interact.

stressor a change that provokes a response in an individual.

stroke rupture of a blood vessel in the brain.

symptom a change in the way your body feels or looks or behaves. It is a sign used by doctors to identify or diagnose illness.

Index

Note on case studies

Photographs illustrating the case studies in this book were posed by models.